William F. Buckley

1969

SIGNS OF THE TIMES
1939–1961

Osbert Lancaster's other volumes

PROGRESS AT PELVIS BAY

PILLAR TO POST

HOMES SWEET HOMES

DRAYNEFLETE REVEALED

THE SARACEN'S HEAD

CLASSICAL LANDSCAPE WITH FIGURES

FAÇADES AND FACES

HERE OF ALL PLACES

Pocket Cartoons

ETUDES

LADY LITTLEHAMPTON AND FRIENDS

STUDIES FROM THE LIFE

TABLEAUX VIVANTS

PRIVATE VIEWS

THE YEAR OF THE COMET

SIGNS
OF THE
TIMES

BY
OSBERT LANCASTER

LONDON
JOHN MURRAY, ALBEMARLE STREET, W.1

FIRST EDITION NOVEMBER 1961
REPRINTED NOVEMBER 1961

Printed in Great Britain by Butler & Tanner Ltd., Frome and London

FOREWORD

A PROFESSIONAL preoccupation with the topical is the surest passport to oblivion, and nothing, not even women's hair-styles nor the music of the late Ivor Novello, dates so quickly as the apt comment.

Situations and personalities, once they are no longer contemporary, are swiftly relegated to a limbo from which, after varying periods, they either emerge as authentically historic, or else sink forgotten into a bottomless pit plumbed only by an occasional thesis-writer from the University of Kansas. What name Achilles assumed among the women is now, we know, only a matter for pointless conjecture, but at least the context is still remembered after four millennia ; whereas, while the name which Colonel Barker adopted among the men may still have a faintly familiar ring for the elderly, few can today recall the episode of which she was the heroine and fewer still respond to the innumerable jokes to which it gave rise. And barely thirty years have passed since that transvestist drama made every headline in the land.

In going through the thousand and more drawings, of which the present collection is a small selection, the author was appalled by the number of occasions on which his own response was a total blank. The joke (if joke there were) may once have been, he optimistically supposed, brilliantly apt, but the point remained irretrievable. Others, based on incidents which at the time had seemed of overwhelming significance, destined to live for ever in the annals of the nation, were still—just—comprehensible, but, deprived of all sense of immediacy, undeniably flat. Who now remembers the Lynskey Tribunal or can recall exactly what it was that Dr Edith Summerskill said about cheese ? Today even the Marconi scandal or Lloyd George's 'two acres and a cow' retain a greater relevance.

The value of the present work, if value it possesses, must lie, therefore, in the record it provides, not of events themselves but of contemporary reaction to them. Jokes about V.1's are today no funnier than those which John Leech made about garotters, but the fact that they were once made may, in both cases, be thought to have an historical interest. And it is only this consideration which has prompted the inclusion of certain poor gibes at the Italians which have today a very poverty-stricken ring but which, when fresh-minted, both the artist and a large proportion of his public thought very funny indeed.

But it is not only in recording the contemporary state of mind, or registering the climate of opinion at a moment of crisis, that the self-confident cartoonist may hope to contribute some faint, barely legible, footnote to the history of his times. If his powers of observation are keen and his hand reasonably adroit, his work should provide abundant evidence of the way people looked at any moment during the period when he was active, and it is with this consideration in mind that the author, remembering the pleasure and instruction he has so often derived from prints by Cruickshank, Leech and du Maurier, illustrating legends which it is very difficult to imagine can ever have held the attention of even the most naïve reader for a single second, has included a number of drawings to which the captions, even to his indulgent eye, seem now a trifle dim.

How far the present volume may be thought to fulfil either of these intentions only the author's elders and contemporaries can rightly judge. For the younger generation he can only hope that from the earlier pages a faint but undeniably period aroma may arise, and that a perusal of the more recent section may perhaps prompt the chastening thought that even the most up-to-date reflection of the contemporary scene is subject to the chilling and inevitable request " Next slide, please " ; and that the Teds, with the Beats close on their heels, are already on their way to join the Bright Young Things, and that winkle-pickers will soon be ranged alongside desert-boots and co-respondent shoes in history's boot-locker.

" Time which antiquates antiquities and hath an art to make dust of all things has yet spared " for a few seconds at least " these minor monuments ", and it only remains for their author to express his gratitude to all those who made their creation and preservation possible. To John Rayner whose initial encouragement and subsequent firm tutelage enabled him to survive his first months in Fleet Street ; to Tom Driberg in whose hospitable column the pocket cartoon first found house-room ; to the long-suffering Arthur Christiansen for loyal support and a toleration of personal vagaries which would have driven many editors round the bend, and to his no less patient and enlightened successor, the present editor of the *Daily Express*, without whose readily granted permission these drawings could not have reappeared ; to George Malcolm Thomson for never failing to arouse the hope that he would one day prove a source of inspiration ; to H.M. Foreign Office in whose time and on whose best cream-laid minute paper so many of the war-time drawings were made ; to John Grey Murray whose careful garnering of the sherds over the whole period alone made possible the appearance of the present collection ; and finally to Lord Beaverbrook who never once in twenty-two years made any attempt by hint or pressure to curb the free expression of his cartoonist's opinions, no matter how manifestly they failed to coincide with his own.

O. L.

"Don't worry, Alfredo, it's purely temporary." 12.i.39

"After all, mon brave, seven army divisions are worth a great many umbrellas." 16.iii.39

"You see, it's all a clever bluff. They're really Spaniards dressed up to look like Italians dressed up to look like Spaniards." 26.i.39

"This year we're taking our holiday between the late spring and early autumn crises." 9.ii.39

"It gives me great pleasure, at a time when the population of our Borough has been enlarged by 50,000, to declare this air-raid shelter open." 25.ii.39

"Of course, Sir John Anderson's steel dog-kennels are all very well, but think of the class of dog we may have to share them with." 8.ii.39

"And please remember, Sir Horace, that your distinctions in civil life mean little or nothing to us in the Auxiliary Fire Brigade." 24.ii.39

" Where are you going to, my pretty maid ? "
" That entirely depends on the Milk Marketing Board, sir," she said.   7.iii.39

" Of course, we must face the fact that Madame X's bird-calls are bound to lose something of their effectiveness on television."   18.iii.39

" There's only one solution : we must by-pass the by-pass."   19.i.39

" Shareholders will readily appreciate the enormous advantage it is for a railway company to have on its board two directors who were personally acquainted with the late Robert Stephenson."   24.iii.39

"I'm sorry, but Herr Doktor Goebbels has just decided that it is, after all, a symbol of non-Aryan pluto-democracy." 14.iv.39

"Well, dear lady, I said all along that you were inclined to brood too much on the European situation." 10.vii.39

"I tell you frankly—if this session is prolonged over Goodwood it'll only give Hitler an undue sense of his own importance." 25.vii.39

25.viii.39

"Gad, ma'am, the type they're send-ing us now aren't half the women their mothers were." 7.xi.39

"All things considered, I think you'd do better in the Wrens." 21.iii.40

"Anybody here from M.I.5 . . . Anybody here from M.I.5?" 28.iii.40

"And may I ask just what makes you think that I should know whether there is any standing room at one-and-six?" 27.ii.40

30.i.40

" You see the trouble is, doctor, not that I snore loudly, but that I snore on a wavering note." 5.ix.39

" Well, if the cranks get the black-out modified, what'll happen to the patriots who've cornered the torch-batteries ? " 6.iii.40

"Don't worry, dear—we all heard that one last war." 19.i.40

" We shall remain strictly neutral and defend our territorial integrity at all costs." 16.iv.40

" I don't expect you'll remember me, but I used to know your father very well." 30.v.40

" Believe me, my dear Carol, when you really get to know him, you'll like him a lot." 2.vii.40

" We do want to fight But by Jingo if we don't ! " 11.vi.40

" It's my belief that the Nazis aren't as bad as they're painted. I'm told they've made Leopold very comfortable." 25.vi.40

" Frankly, General, I'm disappointed in the Rumanians." 29.vi.40

"What a pity they went and pulled down the Bastille. It would have come in very useful just now." 13.vii.40

" Heil Hitler ! Feelthy postcards ? " 13.viii.40

"All clear, gentlemen, please!"
30.viii.40

"Yes, we find our services running far more smoothly since we adopted a system of volunteer spotters." 23.ix.40

"Come, come Harriet, remember Drake!" 10.ix.40

"I don't think it can be all over yet, dear.. They've not sounded the warning." 29.viii.40

" The First Lesson is taken from the Book of the Prophet Jeremiah. In view of Section 39B (a) of the Defence Regulations, we will omit it." 24.vii.40

" Funny, I thought we told the Home Office to pull him in weeks ago." 2.viii.40

" Who goes there? Give your answer in triplicate!" 30.x.40

" Of course at the moment it's still just a suspicion." 31.iii.41

"... a stranger from overseas will shortly effect a big change in your position ..." 12.xi.40

"Tell me, officer do you believe in reincarnation?" 20.iii.41

"Ah-ha! As I thought, there's an unexploded nerve in this crater." 28.i.41

" Er, very praiseworthy, Miss Fan-
shawe, but wouldn't it perhaps be
better to write it in Russian ? "
30.ix.41

23.vi.41

" Listen ! I've found a man who
can make the Internationale sound just
like ' Home, Sweet Home '." 17.vii.41

" Which are we, Carruthers—
workers, peasants or intellectuals ? "
18.vii.41

"You stoppa da grumbling. If it hadn't have been for me you'd never have hadda no Empire to lose."
18.xi.41

"I dessay it's different in the Isle o' Capri, but in Shepton Mallet we don't 'ave no siesta hour." 19.i.42

"Well, Antonio, aren't you pleased that the tourist season's opened again?"
4.v.42

"Ah, you youngsters haven't the stamina of old Caporetto veterans like myself." 2.xii.40

" Sergeant ! Look at all this
hair ! "   9.i.41

" Shall we join the gentlemen ? "
26.vi.40

" Fine sights we shall all look in
berets ! ! "   26.iv.43

" A fat lot of use you're going to
be dealing with a mechanised break-
through when it takes you twenty
minutes to stop a taxi ! "   4.xi.42

" Frankly, Meadows, can you see *me* in a utility suit ? " 24.iii.42

" If you're waiting for a No. 73, and I'm waiting for my catsmeat ration and she's waiting to see ' Gone with the Wind ' what sort of queue is this any-way ? " 3.x.42

" I'm assuming, Sir Lancelot, that the abolition of the basic ration applies solely to motor spirit ? " 8.iv.42

" If it weren't for the ' Bundles for Britain', I should be stark naked." 7.vi.41

"Your grandfather wore it at
Rorke's Drift. Gird it on and never
let it leave your side!"   10.i.42

"That, I understand, is the Reiche-
nau of the A.T.S."   2.ii.42

"Tell me, Achmed, what shall I do?
My first wife is pro-Darlan, my second
is pro-de Gaulle and all the rest want to
go to England to join the Home
Guard!!"   15.xii.42

"It's a great pity the Americans haven't got a House of Lords. Why, Admiral, if you'd been in command at Hawaii we'd have made you Lord Pearl Harbour and all this distasteful publicity would have been avoided." 26.i.42

"All our information goes to show that not only are the enemy's lines of communication become dangerously extended, but also the treads of his elephants are wearing out." 26.iii.42

"I repeat, Sir, the Japs are no sports-men—it's always been clearly understood that these jungles are strictly impenetrable." 20.i.42

" Guess what the Führer's going to put in your stocking this Yuletide, Herr General ? ! " 24.xii.42

" If you say ' The days are beginning to draw in ' once more, Herr Oberst, you're for Dachau ! " 15.ix.42

" The official military spokesman stated in Berlin today that the war in the East has now entered a more mobile phase." 9.i.43

S.T.—B

" Would you say, Hercule, that the General looks like resigning or just resigned ? " 16.vi.43

" Vive le Général Giraud ! Vive l'Amiral Darlan ! Vive le Maréchal Pétain ! Vive le Général de Gaulle ! Vive le Uncle Tom Cobleigh ! " 19.xi.42

" This time, mes gènéraux, could you please hold it just a moment longer ? " 24.vi.43

" Of course not ! I just travel purely for the fun of the thing ! " 22.xii.42

" Excuse me, Canon, but I rather think you've liberated my matches." 7.x.44

" Sir Louis is a little despondent this morning—last night he lost the whole of his month's sweet coupons on a single rubber." i.iii.43

"Look, pilotless!"   17.vi.44

"Don't be silly, Horace—there isn't any stinking brute there for you to lay your hands on!"   19.vi.44

"I'm not denying that there may be a split in the German High Command. All I say is that G.O.C. Pas de Calais seems to be fanatically loyal."   22.vii.44

"The 6.20 from Exeter and the West of England, due on Platform Five, will be 35 minutes late . . . On the other hand, unless my ears deceive me, the 6.15 from the Pas de Calais will be dead on time."   26.viii.44

" To the accompaniment of thunderous applause from the vast audience of war workers, Herr Reichsminister Goebbels is now slowly approaching the platform." 6.ii.43

" Sometimes, Ulrich, I get so depressed that even thinking about the next war doesn't cheer me up." 20.iii.44

" Breeding will tell, Herr Graf—*he* didn't outstay his welcome." 24.vii.44

" Quite between ourselves, General, was it you who were responsible for that very funny joke about 'I can't give you anything but Lvov, Baby'?" 8.iv.44

12.vii.43

"It's all very well, Ethel, but you realise that now the trains will never run on time?"   30.vii.43

"The management regret to announce that there will be some last-minute changes in the cast in the final act."   27.vii.43

"I no minda da '*co*'—it's da bit about '*belligerency*' I donta care for." 2.x.43

" We had a splendid rag in the Lords today—chaffing Willy Littlehampton on being a prohibited area ! " 14.iv.44

" I tell you, all this talk about Hastings is deliberate bluff—I know it's Ilfracombe ! " 8.v.44

8.x.42

" At the thard stroke eet will be the eleventh hour precaisely ! " 10.v.44

"All right, all right, I *do* remember that June night in '39 when the band played ' Parlez Moi d'Amour ' at the little bistro on the quai . . ." 18.viii.44

"Among the hitherto secret weapons which the British are using in this invasion is one they call Shaef." 9.vi.44

"He says he thinks the Führer has lost the war and that he personally has always believed in the existence of the Other Germany." 22.viii.44

"I expect she'll think twice before walking out with a Dachshund another time." 15.ix.44

"I hope, Wainscote, you'll be a little
more careful than you were in 1918.
Next time we don't want to find them
full of moth again."   13.ix.44

"Except for 32 squatters, 16 typists left behind by the Ministry of Food, an escaped P.o.W. and some bats, the 'ole place is as silent as the grave." 13.ix.46

5.xi.46

"Have I ever shown you how we used to make tea in the Desert?" 8.viii.46

"Find out what the accused intends to do with his flat for the next two years." 18.ix.46

"One can't even put one's head in a gas-oven with the smallest prospect of success." 31.i.47

"Once and for all, Martha, will you kindly stop asking what I would have done had my flagship sprung a leak in mid-Atlantic?" 4.ii.47

"Brightly shone the moon that night,
Tho' the frost was cruel,
Extra brightly just to spite
The Minister of Fue-oo-el." 24.12.46

"My subject this afternoon is 'Some recent developments in high-tension molecular fission and their application to modern industry'." 8.ii.47

" Fine fools we should have looked if we'd gone to the Savoy last night."
18.iii.47

" 'Pon my word, Miss Dalrymple, the switch-on has certainly brought back the roses to your cheeks."   4.iii.47

7.ii.47

" s–u–n—sun !   Remember ? "
27.ii.47

"Hilda ! Why don't *we* ?"
29.iii.47

"It's a funny thing, but only last night my wife was saying she wondered if there was any opening for her on the Third Programme." 13.xii.46

"You mark my words ! A few more days of this and the Government'll start telling us: 'Less Water Now Means Better Living Sooner'." 31.v.47

"My dear Ethel, if you had ever studied economics you would realise that it's only the fact that things are more expensive which makes you *think* the cost of living has gone up." 23.v.47

"He says it's a sort of reflex that operates automatically every time a Cabinet Minister opens his mouth." 3.vii.47

"Hindustan . . . Pakistan . . . Hindustan . . . Pakistan . . ." 19.vi.47

—"I know it sounds priggish but as soon as ever I get the time I'm *determined* to read some of the Bills we've passed this afternoon." 14.v.47

"I suppose you realise, Calfsfoot, that if we do de-requisition all this land, we shall only encourage a howl for men to be released to till it?" 22.viii.47

"Whatever Mr. Dalton may say, Horatio, it's my opinion that the cheap money period is drawing rapidly to a close." 26.ix.47

"Just to think—this time next Thursday and we shall all be civil servants!" 30.xii.47

"Darling, if anyone from the Ministry of Labour hears him he'll be directed into a steel foundry before you can say Liszt." 21.viii.47

"Charlotte, darling, you don't think Mr. Isaacs would be such a meanie as to direct a girl before she'd finished the job in hand, do you?" 16.ii.48

"If you ask me, Maudie Littlehampton is wearing one of her husband's old parachutes." 18.vi.47

"As an idle hanger-on, I'd swop the Court for the National Coal Board tomorrow—more money, extra petrol and not so hard on the feet." 19.xii.47

"As I told Maudie Littlehampton, one would never *dream* of dressing up like this if one didn't think one was helping the export drive." 24.i.48

"Salisbury can compromise if he likes, but I shall stop at nothing to defend my rights—even if it means going up to London to do it." 6.ii.48

"If Mildred isn't a bit more careful about her friends, she'll end up as partridge en casserole at 8s. 6d. a go before you can say Strachey." 6.xii.47

"Everywhere one goes this year it's the same old story—too many robins chasing too few crumbs." 13.xii.47

"Archdeacon or no Archdeacon, a Doctor of Divinity still ain't a doctor within the meaning of the Act." 14.i.48

"Come now, Mrs. Fontwater, isn't it about time you started shedding-the-load?" 28.x.48

"Willy Littlehampton says that if taxation increases any further he's decided to present himself to the National Trust as a monument of historic importance." 15.viii.47

"Well, Marshdamp, still as keen as ever on a Western Union?" 7.vi.48

"Are you proposing to come in to lunch or do you expect me to bring you some sandwiches on the course?" 17.v.47

30.x.46

"I've just made the intewesting discovewy that Mr. Bevan's national teeth aren't weally up to coping with Mr. Stwachey's national beef." 6.vii.48

"M.P.s can talk about a medical black market as much as they like, but if anyone thinks I'm going to take on Willy Littlehampton's duodenals for five bob a year, they're crazy." 21.vii.48

"But, darling, would Mr. Pollitt
mind *very* much if Belsize Park went
ahead and affiliated itself to the Com-
inform all on its own?" 16.x.47

"Matthew, Marx, Luke and John,
Bless the bed the Dean lies on
—Rather neat, don't you think,
Canon?" 18.xii.47

"Well, last year it was 'The Wages
of Sin', but this time I've painted out
the baby and called it 'Red typist
expelled from the Stationery Office'."
1.iv.48

7.vi.49

"If young Worplesdon goes on much more about 'the New Look' there's going to be dirty work after evensong." 9.i.48.

"Carissima mia, either you supporta da Musicians' Union or I wrecka your encore. See?" 5.iii.48

"I'm afraid there's no doubt about it, Clarence—it's a stay-in strike." 22.i.48

"Now, Runcible, let us see whether this year we can't get right through 'Adeste Fideles' without my having to speak to anyone about hogging the mike." 20.xii.48

" Now, children, keep close behind mother, and if any of you feel tempted to stray just remember poor Uncle Henry who flew over the Soviet Sector." 23.viii.48

" Well, dear, as that's going to be the last cab we shall see for a long, long time, you'd better make sure we get it." 17.vii.48

" Look here, I don't want to sound unduly alarmist, but I don't mind telling you on the strict Q.T. that your Aunt Daphne expects to be completely re-fitted and put back into commission any moment now." 24.ix.48

" I don't care how much we're insulted by Vishinsky, or double-crossed by Peron, or patronised by Eire —but what I will not stand is being whined at by the Burgomaster of Berlin !" 15.xii.48

" Now, by courtesy of the Ministry of Agriculture, Muriel herself is coming to the microphone to confess to you that she is quite unable to distinguish between Government-controlled, pre-fabricated National cattle-cake and the finest grass." 24.i.49

". . . for the 'Coach and Horses' read 'The Nationalised Transport Workers'; for 'The Marquis of Granby' read 'The Regional Commissioner'; for 'The Crown' read 'The State'; for 'The Goat and Compasses' read 'The New Statesman and Nation' . . ." 16.xii.48

" Excuse me, sir, but I wonder if you would mind answering a few personal questions in connection with a rather important piece of research sponsored by the Ministry of Labour ? " 25.x.48

"CAVE—Ministry of Food!" 9.xi.48

"We thus start upon another stage in the magnificent struggle of our people to overcome crushing difficulties etc., etc." 20.ix.49

"Honesty compels me to tell you that the only dark man who is coming into your life in the near future is Sir Stafford Cripps." 17.iii.49

" We dockers——" 12.vii.49

"Once and for all, Engels, if Professor Haldane says it's never as hot as this in the People's Democracies, it *isn't* as hot as this in the People's Democracies, so stop asking deviationist questions." 5.vii.49

"It's a fine state of ecclesiastical affairs when the Dean of Canterbury believes everything he reads in Pravda, and the Bishop of Birmingham doesn't believe half he reads in the Bible." I.iii.49

s.t.—c

"Remind me, some time, to tell you a very funny story about Cardinal Mindszenty." 25.viii.49

"Before taking you over to the
theatre for tonight's performance of
'The Beggar's Opera', I want you to
try to imagine that we are back in 18th-
century London, a London infested
with highwaymen and footpads, and
not a single policeman——" 4.i.49

30.viii.49

"Now, on Saturday, Sanguine,
you're going to keep your eye firmly
fixed on the man in front, and just
forget that such a thing as television has
ever been invented." 25.iii.49

" Once and for all, Alfred, will you please realise it's practically no comfort to me to be told ' We've got something far, far nastier up our sleeves.' " 24.ix.49

"Well, gentlemen, we are agreed then, that the trivial risk of dissolving the solar system must be subordinated to the higher interests of scientific truth and our researches will continue?" 31.i.50

" Sometimes I can't help wondering just how long it'll be before rather similar stories start appearing in the Martian Press." 28.i.50

"I may be underestimating slightly, but on my reckoning this makes the seventeenth 'most important mission in history' since 1945." 1.ix.49

"Aristocratic, uncontemporary and effete I may be, Senator, but *privileged*— NO ! ! !" 2.xi.49

"Darling, how does one entertain Americans ? . . . If one gives them Spam and doesn't change, we're a down-at-heel, C3 nation, dying of malnutrition, while if one blows the week's meat ration and wears a new frock one's shamelessly abusing Marshall aid !" 12.xi.48

"Turn left where it says 'No cigarettes', keep straight on past wot used to be the petrol pump till you sees a notice saying 'No admittance by order of the War Office', and that's the old Elizabethan Manor 'ouse." 25.viii.48

"I don't want to sound unduly depressing, Brigadier Pasha, but you remember what happened last time we tried out the strategy of allowing the Israelites to reach the Red Sea unopposed?" 5.i.49

"I suppose that now we've been nominated Miss Groundnuts 1949 it would be beneath our dignity to help with the washing-up." 12.i.49

"Try if you like, cher ministre, but I'll bet you he's got a clause in his contract forbidding him to form a Government." 9.ix.48

S.T.—C*

"Miss Wackenbacker, the chairman wants you to drop everything and go right out and buy a large crystal ball." 4.xi.48

" Oh, we're enjoying every minute of it—he's bitten the Tory, been sick over the Socialist and now I can hardly wait to see what he's going to do to the Liberal ! " 20.ii.50

"Darling, doesn't it strike you as rather sinister that so far nobody seems to be making any effort to attract the Upper-Class vote ? " 30.i.50

" And what sort of civil servant is this dear little fellow going to be when he grows up ? " 11.ii.50

"I assure you, miss, that no one's more eager than I am to 'hold the scales evenly balanced' but, try as I may, I can just never remember what Mr. Attlee looks like." 12.i.50

"I should rather think, Heavy-weather, that you and I are the only two voters left with a first-hand-knowledge of half the issues being discussed in this election." 21.ii.50

"Eeny—meeny—miney—mo—catch —a—nigger—by—his—toe——" 23.ii.50

"Well, well, Filebrace, now that our Minister can't leave the House for a split second you and I will at least be able to govern the country without amateur interference." 28.ii.50

"By the way, Gilderoy, wasn't it you who were saying that you'd welcome a small majority as likely to lead to a healthy quickening of Parliamentary life?." 10.iii.50

" Why, your Excellency, I promise you I've been looking forward to a long, cosy chat ever since my husband told me the Diplomatic Corps have practically *unlimited* petrol ! " 7.iii.50

" Patience, patience, Enrico —with any luck they'll start shedding the load just as she reaches top E." 5.i.51

" Immediately after the Nine o' clock News, Mr. Isaacs will speak on ' The menace of unofficial strikes.' " 27.ix.50

" Allow me to remind you, Miss Maltravers, that if Michelangelo had knocked off work every time there was a trifling power-cut the Sistine Chapel would never have been finished ! " 23.xi.51

"Before starting on the agenda may I ask just once more—is there *no one* present who can let our chairman have change for a pound?" 2.vi.50

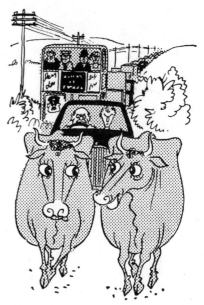

"Honestly, I've not managed to work up a queue like this since I was quite a tiny calf!" 31.v.50

"Now if only they'd arrange Royal Visits to coincide with the Lord Mayor's Show and the Opening of Parliament one could abandon all thought of moving and spend the day quietly in bed!" 22.xi.50

" Lady Littlehampton sends her love and please do you think the Russians will move before Goodwood ? "   30.vi.50

"Just as one was beginning to feel that France was herself again, with three Governments a week, those wretched Koreans must needs go and start a rival crisis."   6.vii.50

" Will one of you boys find out from Butch how much it's goin' to work out in increased footage if we substitute ' Russian-sponsored Communist North Koreans ' for ' Japanese ' throughout ? "   3.vii.50

"How right you were, dear, when you said it had been just like a pre-war weekend ! "   27.vi.50

" Do you think it would be rather escapist if we left after the next over and listened to the news ? " 29.vi.50

" Oh dear, I'm afraid things are getting really serious, Maudie Littlehampton's got that old 1939 of-course-my-lips-are-sealed-but -I'm-really-working-for-M.I. 5 look." 19.vii.50

" That's right, you old masochist, turn on the news and let's have a real good laugh ! ! ! " 6.xii.50

" How times have changed ! When I first joined the Foreign Office it was we who started wars and the military who finished 'em ! " 29.xi.50

"Just a moment, comrade! How about a beautiful souvenir portrait to take back to show the fellow-workers?" 24.vii.50

"What I particularly resent about the Government's policy towards scientists is the implication that we are not wholly trustworthy." 23.v.50

"Never forget, my boy, that in a democracy the will of the majority must always prevail, even when they're in a minority." 1.viii.50

"Excuse me, Mr. Picasso, but the secretary of the delegation of East Surrey Lower Fifth-form Fighters for Peace wants to know if you will draw a pig with your eyes shut in her autograph book?" 14.xi.50

" No, no, Therese, your price is too high—I cannot betray the plans of my country's Festival ! ! " 20.x.50

" There's a strikers' demonstration coming in from the north, a housewives' protest march advancing from the west, a monster rally at the Albert Hall, a giant elm going to the Festival, and the lights have stuck." 9.iii.51

" Please, exactly which building is it that is going to be sent to Coventry and turned into the new cathedral when the exhibition's over ? " 27.ix.51

"Darling, just point me out the Palace of Groundnuts and the Gambia Egg Pavilion." 28.iv.51

27.iv.51

"Anything he can do I can do better." 21.vi.51

"It's not that I'm defeatist, Achmet, it's just that I can't get rid of an uneasy feeling that this has been tried before." 18.v.51

17.v.51

"There you go, never giving a thought to listener reaction—now I ask you is this the time or place for 'In a Persian Market'?!" 27.vi.51

"That should teach them!" 15.ix.51

"For heaven's sake stop saying 'at least *our* Ministers don't burst into tears'—there are moments when it would make a lot more sense if some of 'em did!" 28.ix.51

"Well, and how's little Miss Mossadeg this morning—still determined to get along without foreign technicians?" 14.ix.51

"Darling Sir George, *do* tell me just what makes you think we've got a foreign policy for the missing diplomats to tell the Russians the secrets of about!" 13.vi.51

"My dear, the moment I saw her badge I said to myself here's another case of faulty screening!" 14.vi.51

"Now why on earth, darling, should you think it's either Burgess or Maclean? For all you know it's just as likely to be our host." 19.vii.51

"But Willy darling, if it's bad form to make jokes about Americans, and tactless to ask diplomats where they're going for their holidays, and breach of privilege to criticise the Government, what on earth IS one going to talk about?!" 20.vi.51

"Oh, by the way, darling, I quite forgot to tell you—the doctor says I've got a slipped disc!" 5.xii.51

"I suppose if I'd told you it was by Sartre you'd have thought it wonderful!" 20.xii.51

"I can quite see why the Americans regard Paul Robeson as an export reject, but *why* hold up the import of Graham Greene?" 2.ii.52

"To hell with artistic integrity—next year I'm going to compromise with my ideals and send to the Academy." 19.viii.52

" —and us still waiting for an Inner Circle as like as not ! "   10.ix.51

" Now if only we can find a Zebra, we can sit down and relax ! "   15.xii.51

" Well, it's certainly a great comfort to know that fares still aren't high enough to make them worth the conductresses' while coming upstairs for ! "   6.iii.52

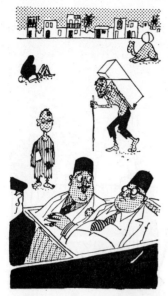

"Have you noticed, Yussuf, how in times of great national crisis class-distinctions become completely unimportant?" 13.xii.51

"I'm rather afraid, Potsherd, that we shall have to revise the Tutankhamen attribution—the first line appears to read : 'There was an old man called Farouk——'" 25.i.52

24.vii.52

"Willy darling, if anything should happen to the Dean of Canterbury, *some people* are going to find themselves faced with a very nasty shortage of raw materials." 28.vii.52

"Was ist's Liesl? Can you not see that I am desperately trying to publish my account of how I led the underground opposition to the last Fuehrer before it's time to start heiling the next!" 9.vii.51

"Surely, darling, there's not such a shortage of up-to-date contemporary crises that they have to start staging revivals?" 6.ii.52

"Why, Sir Archibald! You don't mean to tell me it's the *same* General Franco people used to get so hot under the collar about when I was quite a little girl!" 26.ii.52

"Excusez-moi, M'sieurs et M'dames—but is there a Prime Minister in the house?" 5.iii.52

"Now it's all perfectly simple—provided you remember never to mention the United States, the Persians, Aneurin Bevan, the cost of living, groundnuts, spectacles, the Colonial Development Corporation, and Mr. Dalton, you've got a completely free hand!" 3.x.51

"Don't you think on the whole, Sir Henry, that most politicians would be wiser just to remain beautiful, disembodied voices?" 19.ix.51

"O Willy darling, please don't be cross, but such a pathetic little man came to the door and asked me to stand as a Liberal candidate that I said 'Yes'." 22.ix.51

1.x.51

" But of course the Liberals believe
in votes for animals ! "   24.ix.51

" Honestly,   don't   you
think it would be rather chic
to be the only constituency
in England to return a
Liberal ? "   18.x.51

" Policy ? But, Mr. Chairman, do we *really* have to have
a policy ?   After all, no one
else has got one."   11.x.51

"Wotcher mean—I look like a floating vote?" 22.X.51

"And gentlemen in England, now abed——" 25.X.51

"SEND ONE HUNDRED FIFTY POUNDS IMMEDIATEST STOP DEPOSIT LOST LABOUR CANDIDATE PONTOON STOP MAUDIE" 13.X.51

"Darling, it's too awful. I was so busy radiating quiet confidence that I completely forgot to vote!" 26.X.51

"I always said it was play-
ing with fire to do 'We Three
Kings from Orient Are' in
costume!"   22.xi.51

"Now *this* year we'll all park our
gats in the porch!"   24.xii.51

Not to use bad language in front of
the children—unless they use it first.
   Always to tell the truth—except on
the telephone.
   Always to try and remember that
civil servants are human beings——
2.i.52

" Speaking at Strasbourg yesterday,
Mr. Eden struck an optimistic note . . .
17.ix.52

" Now is the time for all good men
to come to the aid of Apartheid. Heil
Malan ! " 24.iii.52

" Every time one looks at a paper
these days one's sense of insecurity
increases." 15.v.52
s.t.—d

" ZUM BEFEHL, HERR GENERAL ! And
when, please, do we receive our atom
bomb issue ? " 26.v.52

"But Willy, you old stupid, if Gigi Pernod-Framboise gives me the money in francs and I lose it back to her at Canasta in pounds, Mr. Butler can't possibly object." 31.vii.52

"Now, Willy, I hope you're not going to be so downright dishonest as to start declaring things just because the Tories are in!" 16.viii.52

24.iii.53

" You didn't need to watch
Philip Harben ! ! You *knew*
how to make crêpes Suz-
ette ! ! ! " 31.i.53

" I say, isn't it wonderful to
think· there'll be no more
chances for Mummy to go
round looking martyred, telling people : ' Of course *we*
always give *our* ration to the
children ' ! " 5.ii.53

" Don't look round now,
Herbert, but I'm afraid something rather beastly has happened." 29.vi.53

" My boy, I want you to
regard this not as a setback but
as a challenge—go right out
and start creating short-
ages ! ! " 6.xi.53

"Well, if you're still wondering why poor Cain turned out the way he did just take a look at these horrid modern cave-paintings." 9.i.53

"Better come away now, dear—you know how madly secretive primitive peoples always are about their tribal magic." 4.x.52

"But, Ali, if it's no nicer one side of the sound-barrier than the other, why go through it?" 25.ix.53

"You mark my words, Fetlock, in the war *after* next they'll be glad of cavalry!" 20.ii.54

"Ssh! Wait for it!"
20.X.52

"Penny for the guy?"
24.X.53

"Well, if only you'd get yourself a job I shouldn't have to make these annual concessions to bourgeois prejudice!!" 12.xii.53

"Didn't I tell you we'd rather die than appear on television wearing our bifocals ! ! " 7.vi.52

"In any case it's certain to work out a whole lot cheaper than going to the Abbey by bus ! " 6.i.53

GROCERI

"And he needn't worry about young Cuthbert knowing the ropes—he's been me page at every Coronation since Edward VII." 28.v.53

"You know—the size which fits into an earl's coronet and still leaves room for a packet of biscuits and an apple ! " 29.v.53

"Willy, darling, come and see how I'm going to look in the Abbey!"

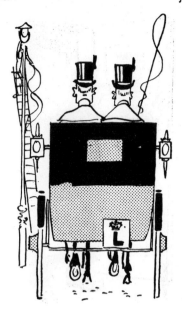

7.v.53

"Darling, what would you say if I were to tell you I'd left the tickets in the cloak-room at the Four Hundred?"
2.vi.53

"How on earth *can* I pick up my skirt when that ghastly little Viscountess in the row behind kicked my shoes out of reach!!"   3.vi.53

" Ah, well ! Back to the
crystal ball ! "   11.vii.53

25.ix.52

" Darling, wouldn't it be wonderful
if just for once somebody, somewhere,
thought it worthwhile to speculate
about what *we* were going to do ? ! ! "
10.iii.53

" —and one final word of advice to
you, officer—remember Beria ! " 5.i.54

"Some of you who have been privileged to hear Canon Fontwater may have been asking what makes his surplice whiter than the Archdeacon's."
19.v.52

"Half measures are no good, we must force the Government to close the museums entirely—they're a gross waste of public money and compete unfairly with sponsored television!"
16.vii.52

"All through the debate there was only one thought in my mind—will sponsored TV help Miss Cheesecake in her career?" 28.xi.53

"—and here is Leonardo's supreme masterpiece—the Mona Lisa!! Are you, too, afraid to open your mouth when you smile?" 20.vi.53

" Tell me, darling, if all that stuff about wise old Mother Nature and natural selection's true, why is it that the girls who run fastest are always those no one's ever going to chase ? "   17.vii.52

"Just the usual holiday routine, Sarge—two Channel swimmers in difficulties, four Girl Guides stuck in a cave, a break-out from the lunatic asylum without bars, and someone's seen a Colorado beetle in the Garden of Remembrance."   26.viii.52

"—and so her two repressed and emotionally unfulfilled elder sisters forced poor little Cinderella to conform to the behaviour pattern of a socially under-privileged domestic worker."   25.xi.52

" But, darling, it's so refreshing to read of a romance where neither of them has ever been married before."   8.i.54.

" To think, my dear Littlehampton, that these are the
fellows who have the nerve
to talk about reforming the
Lords." 1.viii.52

" I suppose it's all really a desperate
effort to try to attract a better class of
Member ! " 17.ii.54

" Let's 'ope yer constituents
don't get to 'ear about this or
yer'll never get that pay
rise ! " 25.iii.54

" At a rough guess I should say that's likely to prove the most unsparkling piece of cross-talk in the whole history of conversation."   6.i.54

"Personally I'm all for secret diplomacy—after all, by this time one's just about *had* open covenants openly not arrived at ! "   10.ii.54

" Oh, just a silly old legend about three monkeys who came here on a good-will visit ! "   28.viii.54

" Don't you provide your Secretary of State with a home ? "   17.ix.54

" Ach, Liesl, what memories those words bring back! You, a slim young thing; me, just demobilised; the factory working overtime . . . ." 22.iv.54

" Brother officers, I give you the toast of the Fifth Freedom—Freedom from Supervision ! ! " 15.vii.54

" Now this morning, children, we're going to learn all about the kindly old flute-player who liberated Silesia." 12.viii.54

" If we really want to rearm Germany, what's wrong with the old system of forbidding her to do it and looking terribly, terribly surprised when she does ? " 29.ix.54

"*Now* who's come un-
stuck?"   7.ii.54

"It's all very well, but one of these
days someone's going to coup d'état
out of turn, and then there'll be
trouble."   16.xi.54

"—and may I remind you, Sergeant-
major, that no one below the substant-
ive rank of captain is permitted by
regulation to form a Government
without previous notification to the
Adjutant."   31.iii.54.

"—and to which beloved
ruler is Allah to be asked to
afford his protection this
morning?"   10.iii.54

"Considering all things, darling, I've come to the conclusion that smoking's worth the risk." 26.iii.54

"I never thought the day would come when I would look to the Budget for light, escapist reading!" 6.iv.54

"I must say it's a fine lookout when there's nothing between us and annihilation but a couple of clairvoyants on the Air Ministry roof!!" 2.iv.54

"I've got an H-bomb, You've got an H-bomb, All god's chillun got H-bombs!" 3.iii.55

"There are certainly a lot
of M.P.s here today!"
16.vi.54

"And now, Comrades, the People's
Melody Makers will play the great
new Soviet song hit: 'How much is
that doggie in the Co-operative?'"
7.i.54

"May I remind you, Lady Littlehampton, that you were not asked to
tell the panel what they could do with
the object, but what it is!"   23.ii.54

" My, my, Mr. Bicker-
steth, aren't you the lucky
one ! ! " 29.xii.54

" I only said—
With a ladder and some glasses
You could see to Hackney marshes
If it wasn't for that so-and-so Citrine."
18.i.55

" In 1962 the train now standing at
Platform 6 will be air-conditioned,
radar-equipped and faster than sound,
but tonight it will be running a leetle
behind time ! " ·29.i.55

" —And you might like to suggest to
the Transport Commission that after
reconsidering your wages they should
toy with the idea of buying some
engines which work in the winter ! "
6.i.55

"You know, darling, there's really something intensely exciting about modern art!" 5.xi.54

"Maxi, you're crazy! Everyone's denouncing horror-comics and you have to go and put a Dali in the window!" 13.xi.54

"Look, Maudie! The poor fella's broken his cast!!" 24.viii.55

"I should say at a guess—one of the younger school." 30.xi.54

'*Lady Littlehampton's only daughter Jennifer, one of the loveliest of the year's debutantes, leaving the Palace yesterday after her presentation.*' 4.iii.55

"—and don't forget what I said about not getting plastered before the Season's properly started!" 8.iii.55

"I dare say Gina Lollobrigida did wear one just like it but Gina Lollobrigida wasn't going to a quiet little dinner dance at the Tetlock-Smythes'." 10.iii.55

"Ernesto's *not* a penniless ice-creamer! He comes of a very ancient Roman family and owns half the Espressos in Knightsbridge!!" 22.iii.55

"Darling, you must meet
my Uncle Bertie — he's
a *genuine* Teddy boy ! !"
20.vii.54

"Well, darling, I've not
actually *read* it, but it's been
a 'must' on my library list
for almost as long as 'Paradise
Lost' and 'The Brothers
Karamazov'." 25.iii.55

"So beastly secretive of
Poppy Wensleydale to go and
have that fascinating divorce
just when there were no
papers !" 22.iv.55

"You see, darling, the real
trouble is that nowadays even
people who haven't got the
means live beyond them !"
3.ix.55

"Thank you, I know all about the importance of mother-love, but if you don't stop pinching my nylons you're going to feel more emotionally insecure and unwanted than you've ever felt in your life ! ! " 14.ix.55

" Of course I realise that to you I'm just a social butterfly, but honestly, Leon, that's not the real me ! " 27.iv.55

"Mummy darling, guess what?—that's me ! ! " 30.iv.55

"For Heaven's sake, child, do at least try and *look* as though you're enjoying yourself ! " 29.iv.55

" Oh, yes, the children are
growing up fast—why, Tor-
quil's just got his first endorse-
ment and Jennifer passed out
at Queen Charlotte's ball ! "
II.V.55

" You know, darling, I'm just a teeny
bit worried about Jennifer these days—
she seems to get so easily overtired."
29.vi.55

22.vi.55

"Been to any good orgies lately?"
23.xi.54

"A fat lot of good a classical education seems to have done you!" 10.vi.55

'Darling Mummy,
Do you remember your saying that the only way really to learn French is to live in a family?...'
20.viii.55

31.viii.55

N.B. The reproduction of this drawing in any Cyprus newspaper will render all concerned liable to a maximum of FIVE YEARS' imprisonment. —BY ORDER. 5.viii.54

" But, Excellency, I've been madly pro-Enosis ever since he gave that *lovely* party in his yacht at Monte Carlo ! ! " 8.ix.55

" But, darling, when you first said the situation couldn't possibly be worse I told you that you were underestimating Mr. Dulles ! " 15.iii.56

" This means that the Government must hang on to Cyprus at all costs, as otherwise there'll be nowhere left for the Socialists to get us slung out from ! ! " 3.iii.56

" The credit squeeze is certainly taking effect—Aggie Mountpleasant is using last year's Fra Angelico with the date scratched out !" 13.xii.55

" All right, darling, if I let you have the new Graham Greene for three pairs of nylons not your size, will you take the Brahms Third Symphony in part exchange for that large bottle of Chanel No. 5 ? " 29.xii.55

" All right, granted you're my true love, do you mind telling me what I'm expected to do with it ?" 20.xii.55

8.xii.55

"Poor Willy's very low! He says he does think that they might at least have waited to launch coronary thrombosis until he'd got over worrying about smoker's lung!" 6.x.55

"I *do* wish the P.M. would make up his mind about the Cabinet reshuffle— the strain of not knowing whom to drop and whom to take up is almost killing me!" 14.x.55

31.x.55

" Well, now we've got the new sports-ground, the handicraft centre and the psychiatric clinic, and have agreed to spend forty thousand on the new swimming pool, it don't seem to matter much whether the teachers strike or not ! " 14.xii.55

" Faites vos jeux, messieurs et mesdames, faites vos jeux ! Rien ne va plus ! ! " 18.iv.56

" One of these days it's going to occur to some intellectual giant in London Transport to embark on the revolutionary policy of collecting fares as well as raising them ! " 6.xii.55

" Unofficial strike 1954, unofficial strike 1955, and a special good conduct medal for five years' continuous service without once stopping at a request stop." 25.xi.55

"Don't let's overdo it, just let's say
'a crazy mixed-up kid'."   23.iii.56

"Now's yer chance, com-
rades! Foller the party line
and win a lovely bowl of
goldfish !!"   2.iv.56

"Although I'm not yet a confirmed
hypochondriac, if I have to hear much
more about the President's intestines I
very soon will be !!"   12.vi.56

"—no sooner had Ali Baba pronounced the magic words 'Open Sesame' than he found himself in an enormous cave packed with Cadillacs, Coca-Cola, and the largest block of oil shares east of Suez !" 18.i.56

"Do you mind just waiting while Mr. Dulles puts Sir Anthony in the picture ?" 13.i.56

"Mr. Van Hamburger, will you please realise, once and for all, that there are certain British assets which will for ever remain beyond the reach of dollar-imperialism ! !" 16.vi.56

"It's all very well the P.M. saying we'll stand by our friends in the Middle East, but what on earth makes him think we've still got any friends in the Middle East ?" 9.iii.56

" According to Freud, deep down inside me there's a father-image with an expense account." 10.v.56

" Oh, to hell with Nancy Mitford ! What I always say is—if it's *me* it's U ! " 1.v.56

" Personally, I regard the case for a capital gains tax as proved ! ! " 23.i.56

"Lady Littlehampton ? " 20.vi.56

" Cheer up, darling—even if they do abolish the death penalty there's absolutely nothing they can do about a fate worse than death ! " 12.vii.56

" Excuse me, but why on earth did you ever give up burning scientists as witches ? " 2.ix.55

" Let me recall the warning I gave when your lordships decided to abolish the rack. ' This,' I said, ' is the thin end of the wedge ' ! " 11.vii.56

"You know, darling, the gossip-writers are quite right —this year the London season really *has* recaptured that pre-war feeling!" 1.viii.56

"Starlings, ma'am? If you ask me they're more likely chickens coming home to roost!!" 4.viii.56

"Sir Anthony Eden when he heard Mr. Dulles was coming!" 2.viii.56

" Your poor uncle is dreadfully depressed—he keeps on
referring to the Canal as some
creek or other and says we
are right up it without a
paddle ! "   16.viii.56

" Goody, goody, goody ! ! ! "
15.viii.56

" I suppose it would be silly to hope
that the Russians might sell the
Egyptians up 'the river before the
Americans sell us ? "   17.viii.56

" I wonder if Colonel
Nasser has ever seen a
nationalised canal ? " 8.viii. 56

"Parliament recalled on Wednesday !? But I always thought they weren't allowed to discuss anything until fourteen days after it had been debated by the T.U.C. !" 8.ix.56

"But, darling, I still don't understand—if that's the way he feels about Suez why ever did he leave it in the first place ?" 13.ix.56

"Nationalised postcards ! Feelthier than ever ! !" 28.viii.56

"Call a top-level Three-Power meeting right now and what do you get? Two convalescents and a drunk !" 23.xi.56

"I wonder, could you possible spare a foolish virgin half-a-gallon?" 4.xii.56

"And now I want some for sending to the States with plenty of holly and not too much about good will!" 1.xii.56

"Unfortunately, that's not the only thing he's stepped in!" 3.i.57

"Of course I know there weren't petrol coupons in Alexander the Great's time—all I said was if there *had* been *he* wouldn't have forgotten them!!" 1.i.57

"*Cave*! Party line's changed!"
19.i.57

"He says you'd better watch your step—*his* tribe had some oilfields once!"   1.ii.57

"What with Hammerskill and Summerskold Scandinavia's certainly got a lot to answer for!"   30.i.57

"Darling, the First Lesson was sheer bliss—all about what happened to the Egyptians when there wasn't any United Nations!!"   19.ii.57

"Same old stuff—Wykehamists of the World Unite!" 12.ii.57

"Really, Jeremy darling, I do think you might have warned me that you'd been posted to G.H.Q., Nato!!" 5.iv.57

"Tell me, Daddy, does one have to be a Communist in order to become an engineer?!" 15.ii.57

"Why can't Mummy get an angry young man of her own to be exploited by?!" 16.iv.57

"Don't tell me if it involves a
breach of security, but just which
continent had you in mind?" 14.vi.57

"But it can't be the
American earth satellite—it's
carrying no advertising!"
4.vii.57

5.xi.57

" A trough of low pressure is moving rapidly eastward across the North Atlantic—and guess who's in it ! "
30.vii.57

" Now I've got a little problem to ask the Foreign Office—if it takes a divided Germany 10 years to get us into the present mess, how long will it take a unified Germany to get us into a worse one ? "   2.x.57

" Unfortunately, in the present crisis too many of our politicians are prepared to go to almost any length to *avoid* the Premiership."   3.x.57

" Comrades ! I give you the toast of ' Absent friends ', coupled with names of . . ."
8.xi.57

" But how on earth do you expect
me to keep my eye on the road *and*
keep up my reading ? " 22.ix.56

" Venus, Greek, second half of the
third century B.C., 41-18-35½ ! "
27.ix.57

" So I give up smoking
and what do I get ? As like
as not Asiatic flu, polio, and a
packet of radio-active fall-
out ! ! " 29.vi.57

" Daddy darling, who's your favour-
ite character in history ? "
" Herod." 15.xi.57

"Has Mr. Hagerty said anything yet about the much bigger one that the Americans have got on the stocks?" 25.i.58

"And why would poor ould Ireland not be having an H-bomb of her own?" 11.xii.57

"Heavens above! Is there absolutely *nothing* that we're still capable of doing for ourselves?" 28.ii.58

"No matter what happens in Paris,
Miss Windrush—you will always be
the Dior of Nuneaton."   14.i.58

"Now there's a pair of
knees that haven't changed a
bit !"   12.ii.58

"Willy ! ! That's *not* funny !"
13.ii.58

"My dear Willy, if only you weren't
so hopelessly out of touch you wouldn't
go leaping to ridiculous conclusions !"
29.v.58

"Please forgive me, Mr. Clam-backer—I'd *honestly* completely forgotten that S-L-U-M-P was a dirty word." 12.iii.58

"You and your jumbo Martinis ! !"
1.iv.58

"If little Elmer asks one more dam'-fool question about Princess Margaret, little Elmer is going to have a very, very traumatic experience !"
5.iv.58

" You know how it is with those Paris politicians, mon general—nothing but talk, talk, talk ! " 22.v.58

" A qui le dites-vous ? ! " 2.xii.58

15.v.58

"If the buses stay out much longer, none of us'll have the money to take them when they do come back." 23.v.58

"—and, Miss Lovejoy, you will remember what we said about the end of the strike not seeing the end of our friendship." 21.vi.58

To the Editor. 'Dear Sir, Writing on behalf of a body of men what has never bin influenced by any consideration of creed or colour, we wish to protest against the use of the term "race gang" to describe a set of ooligans fer whom we as nothink but contempt.' 6.ix.58

"Heads we go to Notting Hill, tails we go to the pictures." 2.ix.58

" —and there was I ready to cry my eyes out because the little rat wasn't in the Honours List ! "   13.vi.58

" —and, finally, never forget that every man carries two volumes of memoirs and a field-marshal's syndication rights in his knapsack ! " 4.xi.58

" Isn't it wonderful ? Since Rudolf slipped a disc he's decided to compromise with his ideals and give up action painting ! "   22.xi.58

13.xii.58

"Darling ! !—O ! I *beg* your pardon ! " 9.i.59

" New on this morning and laddered before Matins ! " 8.vii.58

" I wouldn't worry, darling —she's probably radar-controlled." 4.ii.59

" As they're obviously none of them going to be on speaking terms by the time they get there, I quite frankly fail to see the point of the climb."   30.vii.58

" Darling, isn't it odd—apparently the Russians have never had it so good either ! "   29.i.59

" Keep your fingers crossed, boys ! Peaceful Co-existence is about to face the acid test ! "   19.ii.58

" One does not wish to sound un-oecumenical, but, really, do they *have* to wear those ridiculous hats ? ! "   21.ii.59

"Darling!! I've a ghastly feeling I've taken the lucky charms and put the tranquillisers in the pudding!" 18.xii.58

"No, no, Ursula dear! Not '*Nymphets* and Shepherds come away'!" 30.i.59

"Willy!! Will you kindly explain just exactly what you meant by that extraordinary remark about shutting the stable door?!" 7.iii.59

"Lolita!" 30.iii.59

S.T.—F

"If my memory's not at fault, we should be hearing about Anschluss any moment now." 7.vii.59

"Watch that right arm, Siegfried!" 30.xii.59

"Ein Märchen aus alten Zeiten,
  Das kommt mir nicht aus dem Sinn."
1.i.60

"Forty years on! Growing older and older!" 6.i.60

"Ah! Maintenant je comprends! In England it does not matter what you do so long as you don't do it in a parked car. Yes?" 23.vi.59

"I'm so dreadfully sorry for the poor little things—they've had to postpone their elopement because of this talk of a newspaper stoppage." 30.vi.59

"And it couldn't have happened at a worse moment —Daphne's ball, Lulu's divorce and Odo Barnstaple coming up on a serious charge!" 2.vii.59

"And, please, dear child, not a word about our golden wedding— your aunt feels that nowadays the fewer people who realise that she's spent fifty years with the same Duke the better." 25.iii.60

" To think we've had to go through all the sweat of electing a new House of Commons and the first thing they start talking about is Suez ! " 31.x.59

" Now please don't ask me why— just accept the fact that the whole situation is quite, quite different ! " 5.xi.59

" Oh, I do so agree ! Of *course* France can't afford to develop a really effective nuclear deterrent—but what's really worrying me is, can we ? " 18.ii.60

"Isn't it strange the way a beret always seems to *do* something to generals."
21.i.60

"I do hope you don't mind my asking, mon colonel, but whose side exactly are the boys who've got charge of that H-bomb on?" 26.i.60

"Well, right now that may mean either half-an-inch on the hemline or barricades on the boulevards!" 28.i.60

S.T.—F*

" Agoraphobia, dear, means fear of open spaces and all the No. 9's have got it badly." 2.xii.59

" So clever old Casanova's had his gondola towed away ! " 16.xii.59

" Would it interest you to learn, darling, that ' our awareness of spiritual values is being gravely impaired by the highest standard of material well-being in recorded history ? ' " 3.ii.60

"Isn't it wonderful?! My dear, when I first heard, you could have knocked me down with a tripod!!" 1.iii.60

"Dr. Meadowsweet!! Allow me to point out that the incurable sentimentality of your sex is liable to involve the whole academic body in baseless charges of snobbery and flunkeyism!" 3.iii.60

"Remember the old days, before we started worrying about those fifteen million viewers, when we did this run in ten minutes flat?" 7.v.60

"All this uncontemporary, escapist stuff is going to look pretty silly when the Anti-Uglies get down this end of the beach." 21.vii.59

"Good heavens! I never realised that anyone felt *that* deeply about Sir John Rothenstein!" 7.viii.59

"What's this in aid of—the Wolfenden Report?" 24.v.60

"Willy, stop !!! A smart left and right and bang goes civilization !" 7.i.60

"Another Christmas, perhaps you'll think twice before giving Aunt Ethel a subscription to the New Statesman !" 19.iv.60

"Mummy's blissfully happy. She's making a list of the first people she'd like to see sent into orbit." 1.vi.60

"For heaven's sake, Maudie, do stop saying 'We've only got K's word for it' and come to bed !" 17.v.60

" Excuse my asking, General, but just how many more of the Dulles brothers are still happily with us ? "   10.v.60

" I shall know that I've had enough, thank you very much, when I can no longer pronounce 'agonising reappraisal'. "   18.v.60

" —to keep Britain and the other allies in good heart by actively demonstrating that the U.S. deterrent force is always on the alert."   20.vii.60

" I know it's terribly, terribly silly, but just recently I seem to have developed a thing about pressing buttons ! "   21.vii.60

" That's what I like about Wyke-hamists—never afraid to wash their old school ties in public." 16.iii.60

" Darling, would one be justified in describing Messrs. Gaitskell and Cross-man as the Argylls of the political world ? " 8.vi.60

" Tell me, darling, does the opposi-tion to Mr. Gaitskell come largely from the native population or just from the white settlers ? " 24.vi.60

"—and your Uncle Arthur's just as pleased as you are—he's not forgotten Ladysmith !" 29.iii.60

" Really, children !   After Mummy gave you that little talk on democracy and world government, too !" 9.viii.60

" Don't say I said so, but I have it on excellent authority that that fellow Tshombe's been whiteballed for Black's !"   10.viii.60

" Do me a favour will you, lady ? Let's leave Mr. Lumumba right out of this." 31.viii.60

"You know, I'm beginning to develop grave doubts as to whether that mare is wholly female..." 24.viii.60

"My forecast for the month is continuous rain and an uninterrupted flow of pictures of female javelin throwers." 19.viii.60

"Are you surprised they're all wolves, considering the way they were brought up?" 27.viii.60

"1, Vatican City; 2..." 30.viii.60

"If it hadn't been for the fact that the bar's in here I should never have got your father past the 'Blue Period'."
7.vii.60

"You know, Conrad, there are moments when I've a nasty feeling that for you I'm just a status symbol."
14.x.60

"Well, it's changed its significance a bit. When it first sprouted it was a demonstration of artistic integrity—now it's a tribute to Fidel Castro." 28.ix.60

"What I particularly admired about the debate was the way that every speaker managed to give the impression that he personally had never met a homosexual in his life." 1.vii.60

"Is anything the matter, Moleskin? You seem so nervous all of a sudden!" 21.x.60

18.viii.60

"An an-gel of the Lord came down
And glo-ry shone a-round."
20.xii.60

" It's quite all right, Willy's
driving so I'm drinking for
two." 22.xii.60

"Willy ! Never mind about John
Peel; d'ye ken Mr. Marples ? ! !"
24.xii.60

" You know, it's an awful thing, but ever since I was a tiny little girl I've never been able to feel as sorry for les braves Belges as I'm sure one should."   30.xii.60

" Sure, they had snow on their boots ! "   5.i.61

" Heavens, how I'd have laughed if it had turned out to be Mrs. Fidel Castro ! " 7.i.61

" Oddly enough, the last time I spoke in this hall Lloyd George was in the chair and the theme was ' Hands off the gallant little Boers '." 8.iii.61

" *You* can call it the death-
wish if you like, but *I* call it
plain, old-fashioned snobbery ! " 24.i.61

" Honestly, Gloria, do we
have to go to the Friendship
for Tigers Rally ? " 27.i.61

" Votes for women 1913, Anti-
blood sports long service medal, Hands
off Abyssinia 1936, Peace Pledge
Union Star, Down with Franco (with
bar) 1937 . . ." 7.iii.61

" Never again do I spend a
nice, quiet week-end in London. On Saturday I tripped
over Bertrand Russell in St.
James's Park, and on Sunday
I was winged by an assegai
in Eaton-square ! " 21.ii.61

"I hope to heaven we *do* launch a satellite in 1961, because then, perhaps, British scientists can concentrate on the apparently insoluble problem of how to get an electric train from point A to point B." 31.xii.60

"Heavens above! Trippers!!" 13.iv.61

"But if space really *is* the Eldorado of the future how come that Mr. Clore and Mr. Cotton haven't gone into orbit years ago?" 4.ii.61

"But, darling Aunt Ethel, supposing the Russians *have* put a man into space, *why* should they want to bring him down in Cadogan-square??" 12.iv.61

"O children! How *could* you?! Why, it might have been Canon Collins!!"
24.ii.61

"'How beautiful upon the mountains are the feet of him that bringeth good tidings'—Isaiah lii. 7."   19.iv.61

"From now on the Rt. Hon. delegates will kindly watch their language!"
15.iii.61

"I'll bet you half my Easter Offering that Font-water's just going to tell us that *he's* got a presentation copy of the original edition signed by the author."
14.iii.61

" It's the Foreign Office—they want to know whether you can possibly remember that frightfully funny story you told them at the time of Burgess and Maclean? " 23.iii.61

" Pomfret, when I gave you that American file and told you what you could do with it, just what *did* you do with it ? " 31.v.61

14.vi.61

"Mais, madame, je *t'assure* que je n'suis pas un Para !" 26.iv.61

"From our point of view, mon General, President Kennedy's kind offer of full assistance to the other side came just too late." 27.iv.61

"But I always said one couldn't expect any *immediate* results—like Mrs. Krushchev dashing straight off to Balenciaga." 6.vi.61

"Fanatically loyal as I am to the Western alliance, I could wish that the White House would stop whistling to keep other people's courage up !" 22.vi.61

"Cousin Constantia says Lord Hinchingbrooke is quite right—if we join the Common Market we shall be landed with the Continental Sunday before you can say Lord's Day Observance Society!" 22.v.61

"Is it true, Sir Caspar, that our invisible exports are now so invisible that've had to call in Jodrell Bank to find them?" 20.vi.61

"Darling, did you realise that the Common Market constitutes a major threat to British cooking?" 24.vi.61

"What's the good of learning to speak the French they speak in France if you can't explain to them that we share their doubts about the Common Market, are 100 per cent sympathetic to their cause and are already two hours late for the ferry?" 27.vi.61

" And what's more, officer, if you're thinking what I think you're thinking you're either a professional contortionist or else you've got a very macabre conception of pleasure ! " 9.v.61

" Once and for all, dear, Mummy knows that whatever it was that the cab-driver called the mini-cab it was a purely technical term." 21.vi.61

" Lord Brabazon, I see, prefers the old, tried methods." 30.vi.61

" That dear, brave, little doggy was never asked to lunch with the Queen ! " 14.vii.61